Tremendous
TRACTORS

To Ben, Joshua, Susie, Justin and Jan.
And to my tremendous editor, Terri – T.M.
For Kelp and Ben – A.P.

The Publisher thanks Pharo Communications at the National Agricultural Centre
in the UK and Charlene Finck (Machinery Editor, Farm Journal) in the
US for their kind assistance in the development of this book.

KINGFISHER
An imprint of Kingfisher Publications Plc
New Penderel House, 283-288 High Holborn, London WC1V 7HZ
www.kingfisherpub.com

First published by Kingfisher 2003
(hardback) 10 9 8 7 6 5 4 3 2 1
(paperback) 10 9 8 7 6 5 4 3 2 1

Text copyright © Tony Mitton 2003
Illustrations copyright © Ant Parker 2003
The moral right of the author and illustrator has been asserted.

A CIP catalogue record for this book is available from the British Library.

ISBN 0 7534 0831 7 (hardback)   ISBN 0 7534 0832 5 (paperback)

Printed in Singapore
1TR/0503/TWP/CG(CG)/170NYM

Tremendous
TRACT

Tony Mitton
Ant Parker

KINGFISHER

ous, chuggy tractors,
dy and so strong,

connecting up to farm machines
and pulling them along.

Their big black tyres have solid treads
which help them not to slip.
These chunky treads can chew the ground
and get the wheels to grip.

A tractor works on farmland,
so its body must be tough.
It sits up high above the ground,
for farmland can be rough.

To grow their crops the farmers
have to start by sowing seed.
But first, to break the ground up,
a plough is what they need.

A tractor pulls the plough
across the field, up and down.
The plough blades cut the soil
into furrows, rich and brown.

crumble

crunch

The tractor hauls the harrow next,
to break the soil some more.

The metal discs crush up the clods –
that's what the harrow's for.

It's time to use the roller now.
The long tube rolls around

to flatten out the field,
pushing stones beneath the ground.

The seed drill has a hopper,
a seed box that you fill.
When it's time for planting,
the tractor pulls the drill.

The seed drill makes a row of grooves
in which the seeds can drop.
The spikes then rake a covering of
soil across the top.

chop
chop
chop

If the crop's a hay crop,
you mow it when it's grown.

The grass is left in tidy rows
to dry, when it's been mown.

plunk

plop

Later on a baler scoops
the stalks up from the ground
and shapes them into bales,
which are bundles, square or round.

A bale of hay is heavy,
so it's very hard to lift.
A bale fork on a tractor
makes it easier to shift.

swish
swish

If the crop's a grain crop,
when harvest time is here
a great big combine harvester
can get the whole crop clear.

psshh!

It cuts the stalks and threshes them
to knock the grain right out,
then spreads the straw behind it,
as the grain spills from the spout.

A tractor with a trailer
shifts bales of straw or hay,
takes food to hungry animals,
or carries crops away.

The tractor and the farmer
work hard and do their best.
So when the day is over
they both deserve a rest.

Tractor bits

tyre

this has chunky **treads** to help the wheel grip bumpy or slippery ground

seed drill

this scratches small grooves in the ground for planting seeds

← **hopper**

this holds the seeds and blows them out through a row of tubes

bale fork

this is for lifting bales of hay or straw and moving them around

blade

a plough has sharp blades, or **shares,** to cut into the ground and turn over the soil

spikes

these move through the ground to cover the seeds after they drop